ISBN 978-0-428-15076-1
PIBN 11249885

English
Français
Deutsche
Italiano
Español
Português

www.forgottenbooks.com

Mythology Photography **Fiction**
Fishing Christianity **Art** Cooking
Essays Buddhism Freemasonry
Medicine **Biology** Music **Ancient
Egypt** Evolution Carpentry Physics
Dance Geology **Mathematics** Fitness
Shakespeare **Folklore** Yoga Marketing
Confidence Immortality Biographies
Poetry **Psychology** Witchcraft
Electronics Chemistry History **Law**
Accounting **Philosophy** Anthropology
Alchemy Drama Quantum Mechanics
Atheism Sexual Health **Ancient History**
Entrepreneurship Languages Sport
Paleontology Needlework Islam
Metaphysics Investment Archaeology
Parenting Statistics Criminology
Motivational

c, Archive Document

assume content reflects current
ic knowledge, policies, or practices.

United States $A\,37$
Department of $o\,2$
Agriculture

Foreign
Agricultural
Service

Circular Series

ATH 5 95
May 1995

Agricultural Trade Highlights

Exports Up 38 Percent in February
Sharpest Increase in Bulk Commodities

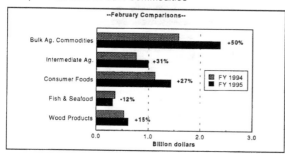

--February Comparisons--

Bulk Ag. Commodities +50%
Intermediate Ag. +31%
Consumer Foods +27%
Fish & Seafood -12%
Wood Products +15%

FY 1994
FY 1995

0.0   1.0   2.0   3.0
Billion dollars

February trade statistics released on April 19 by the Commerce Department placed the value of U.S. *agricultural, fish, and forest product* exports at $5.8 billion, a 31-percent increase over the February 1994 level. Agricultural exports alone totaled $4.8 billion, up 38 percent over year-ago levels with bulk, intermediate, and consumer-oriented exports each registering double-digit gains. Fish and forest product exports totaled $941 million in February, up 4 percent from the same month last year.

February's shipments bring the five month year-to-date total for agricultural, fish, and forest product exports to $27.4 billion, 20 percent higher than the same period last year. Agricultural exports were the best performers, growing 22 percent over last year to $23.3 billion. Performance continues to improve for bulk, intermediate, and consumer-oriented products registering gains of 26, 20, and 19-percent, respectively over last year. Exports of fish and forest products grew 6 percent over the first five months of last year to $4.1 billion.

At $2.4 billion, U.S. exports of *bulk commodities* increased 50 percent in February over a year ago. All nine product categories in this sector rose with the sharpest gains seen in cotton, coarse grains, and wheat. Exports of U.S. cotton increased 242 percent, continuing to reflect sharply higher sales to China. Coarse grain sales were 64 percent higher than February of last year while wheat exports were up 32 percent. During the first five months of the new fiscal year, bulk commodity exports totaled $10.8 billion, up 26 percent over the same period last year.

U.S. exports of *intermediate products* reached $1 billion in February, up 31 percent from the same month last year. Gains were fairly broad-based with the strongest gains being registered in vegetable oils, animal fats, and hides and skins. These increases more than offset a 25-percent decline in live animal exports. For the first five months of fiscal 1995, intermediate product exports are up 20 percent to $4.9 billion and appear to be headed for a new record high in 1995.

Despite continued slow sales to Mexico, worldwide exports of U.S. *consumer-oriented products* continued to rise in February, with sales totaling $1.4 billion, 27 percent ahead of levels during the same month last year. Gains were broad-based with the most significant increases recorded in chilled and frozen red meats, poultry meat, processed fruit and vegetables, and tree nuts. February's performance brought consumer food exports for the first five months of fiscal 1995 to $7.6 billion, up 19 percent from the same period in fiscal 1994. Like intermediate products, consumer foods are clearly headed for a new high.

At $365 million in February, edible *fish and seafood* exports fell 12 percent over the same month last year. The largest decline was registered in crab and crabmeat. U.S. fish and seafood exports finished the first five months of fiscal 1995 at $1.1 billion, up 6 percent from the previous year. February was a good month for U.S. *forest product* exports, rising to $620 million, up 15 percent from last year. Exports in all four forest product categories were up but logs accounted for the majority of the gain. In the first five months of fiscal 1995, U.S. exports of forest products rose 7 percent over year-ago levels with shipments totaling almost $3 billion.

U.S. Agricultural, Fish and Wood Export Summaries
October-February and Latest Month Comparisons   ■ FY '94   ■ FY '95

Product Summary

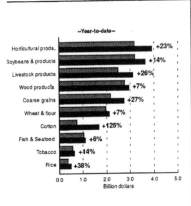

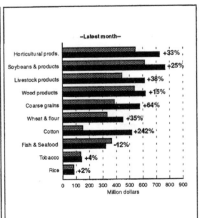

Top Ten Markets Summary

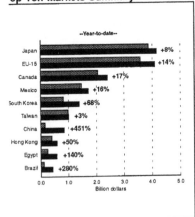

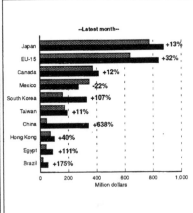

Note: Percentages are computed as the change from a year ago.

Consumer Food Highlights

U.S. consumer food exports totaled $2.7 billion for the first two months of 1995, an increase of 18 percent compared to the same period last year. Categories with double-digit growth were chilled and frozen red meats, poultry meat, fresh vegetables, processed fruit and vegetables, juices, wine and beer, and pet food. Increases were also registered for breakfast foods, fresh fruit, tree nuts, and nursery products.

U.S. shipments of *chilled and frozen red meats* in the first two months of 1995 reached $570 million, a 25-percent increase over the same period last year. Aided by the strong yen, Japan continues to be the major factor driving the increase in U.S. red meat exports. Sales have risen 31 percent to $339 million in the first two months of this year. While beef remains the largest component of red meat exports to Japan, pork exports are rising at a faster rate. Reflecting the impact of the peso devaluation, and economic austerity measures which have reduced the buying power and size of the Mexican middle class, shipments of red meat to Mexico reached only $33 million, a 43-percent drop from the same period in 1994.

U.S. *fresh fruit* exports were $272.6 million during the first two months of 1995, eight percent ahead of last year at this time. A slight dip in sales to Canada ($63.6 million) was more than offset by a nearly 40-percent increase in exports to Japan ($86 million). Growth to Japan has been led by grapefruit, oranges, and lemons. While fresh fruit sales to both Taiwan and Mexico experienced a sharp drop during the period compared this time last year, exports are 21 percent ahead to the EU-15 (led by the UK, France, and the Netherlands), 4 percent ahead to Hong Kong, 29 percent ahead to Singapore, 81 percent ahead to Indonesia and 43 percent ahead to Thailand.

Exports of *processed fruit & vegetables* totaled $292 million in the first two months of 1995, 21 percent higher than the same time period last year. There was strong growth to nearly all regions. Japan, the EU-15, the 4-Tigers, and ASEAN-4 all had sales growth ranging from 21-67 percent. Exports to North America were led by 15-percent growth in sales to Canada, reaching $56 million, which offset a 28-percent decline in sales to Mexico.

U.S. exports of *prepared and preserved red meats* were $35 million for the first two months of 1995, off seven percent compared to the same period last year. While shipments to Canada, the largest market, were roughly unchanged from last year, exports to Mexico experienced a sharp decline of 46 percent in the continued aftermath of the peso devaluation. Modest declines in processed red meat sales also occurred to Japan, South Korea, and Hong Kong. The Russian market was one of the few bright spots among the leading markets, with exports gaining 48 percent during the period.

U.S. *poultry meat* exports totaled $272.4 million for the first two months of 1995, a 45-percent increase over the previous year. Frozen chicken cuts were the largest growth item globally. Russia is the leading market at $75.3 million, more than twice the level of last year at this time. Poultry exports to Hong Kong also rose sharply during the period, along with a 5-percent increase to the EU-15, a 23-percent increase to Japan, an 86-percent increase to Korea, and a 158-percent increase to China. Rounding out the top ten markets, sales were lower during the period to Mexico, Canada, Poland, and Singapore.

Snack food exports in the first two months of 1995 totaled $154 million, 3 percent less than the same period last year. The fall in snack food sales is largely due to a decline in sales of baked goods and candy to Russia and Mexico. The bright stars in snack foods continue to be corn and potato chips. Chip sales rose 12 percent to $34 million for the first two months of 1995 compared to the same period last year.

Exports of *wine & beer* totaled $86 million in the first two months of 1995, 70 percent higher than the same period a year ago. Beer exports are rising at a rate of 102 percent compared to last year, reaching $57 million for the January - February period. Continuing the trends from 1994, rising U.S. beer sales are a global phenomena. A strong yen and strong thirsts have led Japan to quaff $13 million of U.S. beer, 43 percent higher than last year. Brazil has emerged as the number two export market with $9 million in sales, 996-percent higher than last year. Wine sales have also continued to rise, reaching $29 million.

U.S. exports of *fruit and vegetable juices* totaled $104.4 million during the first two months of 1995, a 61-percent increase over the same period the previous year. Canada was the leading market with sales of $29.4 million, 13 percent higher than last year. Other markets showing double-digit growth included Japan, South Korea, Hong Kong, and Taiwan. Triple-digit growth was registered to the EU-15, led by Belgium-Luxembourg, France, the Netherlands, and the U.K. Marketing efforts for single-strength orange juice by Florida citrus growers continue to be a significant factor.

Pet food exports totaled $95 million, 15 percent higher than in the first two months of 1994. Sales continue to rise in most markets except for the EU-15, where import restriction proposals may be partially responsible for a slight decline in trade. Exported to Japan rose 44 percent to $27 million compared to the same period last year. Pet food continues as one of the few rising consumer food products being shipped to Mexico this year, rising 19 percent to $4.9 million in the first two months of this year.

For more information, contact Karen Halliburton at (202) 690-0553.

Top Five Markets for Selected U.S. Consumer Foods
February Comparisons

CY '94   CY '95

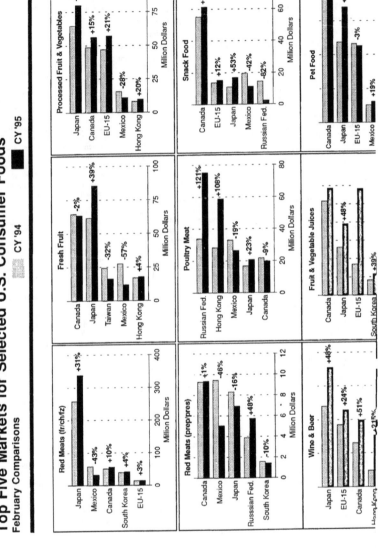

U.S. Frozen French Fry Exports Approach $200-Million Record in 1994

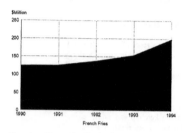

French Fries

U.S. exports of frozen french fries reached a record $199 million in 1994, a 29-percent increase over the previous year's level. Sales have grown an average 17 percent over the last six years, with eight of the top twelve markets at new record highs in 1994. Japan accounted for more than half of global sales ($104 million), registering a 17-percent increase over 1993. High double-digit growth also occurred in South Korea ($12.8 million), Hong Kong ($9.3 million), Mexico ($9.6 million), Taiwan ($7.4 million), Singapore ($5.7 million), Philippines ($7.3 million), Malaysia ($7.2 million), Thailand ($2.2 million), and Indonesia ($2.7 million).

Sales have been linked to the continuing popularity of American fast food overseas. The spread of family-style restaurants which serve french fries with entree dinners has further boosted demand. Evidence of more mainstream diffusion is the availability of frozen french fries and other potato products in supermarkets and wholesale warehouse clubs. The number of households with refrigerators to accommodate home storage of the product has increased throughout Asia, and microwave ovens are also becoming more commonplace.

China is a rapidly growing market for U.S. french fries with huge untapped potential. Much of the product enters the country through southern China via Hong Kong where it is repackaged and then re-exported. The fact that french fries can be prepared in a wok makes an easy transition for Chinese consumers from restaurant consumption to home use. This may explain why frozen french fries were among the first frozen foods from the U.S. to appear in China's newly established supermarkets. Even microwave brands now have a market presence.

U.S. Ice Cream Exports Jump to Record $83 Million in 1994

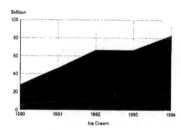

Ice Cream

U.S. ice cream exports posted a 24-percent gain in 1994 to reach a record $83 million. Japan remained the largest market, accounting for one-third of total sales ($27.7 million). Other record-setting markets in the Pacific Rim included South Korea ($2.4 million), Taiwan ($1.8 million), and Singapore ($1.5 million). Consumers are reported to have a preference for U.S.-produced ice cream over its Asian counterpart. Apparently, U.S. ice cream has a richer taste because it is higher in butterfat content than the Asian-produced product which is often substituted with palm oil

Records were also set in Mexico (13.9 million) and the Russian Federation ($6.8 million). Unfortunately, Mexico's peso crisis is expected to limit ice cream sales to that market in the near-term. Prospects for continued exports to Russia may not be sustainable as well. Mars, the primary exporter of ice cream novelty products to Russia, is in the process of building production facilities outside of Moscow.

Although still the third largest market, sales to the European Union fell by 18 percent last year to $11.2 million. Shipments to France ($6.6 million) were off 17 percent, while those to the United Kingdom ($4 million) declined 26 percent. The movement of Haagen-Daz production facilities to Europe has contributed to the drop, and will likely have a long-term impact.

U.S. Condiment Exports at Record $331 Million in 1994 -- Salsa Among the Ho

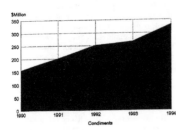

U.S. condiment sales soared to a record $331 million in 199 higher than in 1993. Records were set in virtually all regic world, and in the top ten markets. At a record $121 milli< the top condiment market, with 37 percent of total U.S shipments flowing to that country. The spread of the] Mexican food to Canada and continued growth in consump' chips has led to a growing demand for salsa. Canadian sa based condiments, including ketchup and salsa, reached million in 1994. Condiment sales reached a record $4 Mexico, $29 million to Japan, $28 million to the EU-12, $ Hong Kong, and $15 million to Saudi Arabia. Rec condiments to the Middle East are due largely to successful Louisiana hot pepper sauces. Other factors are the spread of fast food restaurants to the Gulf States.

Global condiment sales have followed the initial spread of fast food restaurants. Now the global expansion of and American regional/ethnic restaurants has created a new demand for condiments. Tex/Mex, Southwest, cuisines have found new popularity in markets as diverse as Paris, Singapore, Hong Kong, and Japan. Anoth rising condiment sales is the global spread of the snacking habit. Potato and corn chip consumption is up arou: and salsa is the perfect accompaniment.

U.S. Lobster Exports Are Boiling at a Record $137 Million in 1994

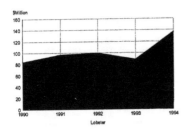

Exports of U.S. lobsters reached a record $137 mill' continuing a spectacular rise from only $5 million i recovering from a drop in export value in 1993. Canada ha EU as the largest market for U.S. lobster, reaching a recor and accounting for two-fifths of total exports. Much of t increase in overall lobster sales from 1993 to 1994 was percent increase to Canada.

The popularity of American (Maine) lobster as a luxury sea spread along with affluence around the world. As a however, it is affected by recessions and economic sluggi slowed sales to the EU and Japan in 1993. Shipments t slowly recovering but have not yet reached the record $54 million set in 1992. Within the EU, France Luxembourg have emerged as bright spots rising to record export levels of $15.8 million and $5.3 million, re

Lobster sales to Japan have bounced back to a record $18.6 million in 1994, a 174-percent increase, aided by t and a strong consumer preference for seafood. Growing affluence and a desire to enjoy it through food consumpt with a tradition of seafood consumption in Taiwan, South Korea and Hong Kong, have led to record export sales $2.3 million, and $2 million, respectively. The spread of affluence throughout the Pacific Rim, including Chi more future market potential for U.S. lobster sales which could reach $220 million if present trends continue, there is sufficient supply.

Feature Story: Target Marketing Consumer Food Products

Why should U.S. companies look beyond the borders of the United States? Food processors may be able to optimize the use of their limited resources by targeting sales abroad, towards markets with less or different competitive pressures. In fact, the most appropriate markets for many firms right now may be outside of the United States. U.S. processed food exporters may find that the global product life cycle framework can be a useful tool in identifying viable foreign market opportunities.

By Carmi Lyon

Many food processing firms assume that the most important and the most viable marketing opportunities are found in the United States. When a substantial consumer foods market is located at your doorstep, why look elsewhere? Even a small piece of the U.S. market could translate into large sales. However, companies ignoring the global market may be missssing important sales and growth opportunities.

Foreign Markets Represent Growth Opportunities

U.S. retail food sales, not adjusted for inflation, have been stagnant, growing only 5 percent annually over the past five years. U.S. exports of consumer foods to all markets have increased 14 percent annually over the same time period. Clearly, most of the growth in consumer food markets is beyond the borders of the United States.

Many U.S. food companies have already discovered that export markets are a better target for investing limited resources because they provide a means for escaping a domestic market that has little potential for growth and is dominated by powerful competitors. Successful firms have chosen target markets by matching company resources with markets that will respond to those resources. Creating this fit can be one of the most overwhelming tasks an exporter faces.

Selecting a target market may be easier with the help of the 'global product life cycle' framework presented by Franklin Root in *Entry Strategies for International Markets (1994)*. Any product or idea goes through a 'life cycle' attracting different kinds of consumers and different levels of competition at each stage. The life cycle starts with a novel product idea consumed by only a few 'innovators,' becomes a commonplace good as it spreads to the masses, and then matures as a new and improved product takes its place.

In applying this framework to foreign markets, consider the conditions that drive markets, placing countries in different stages of the life cycle for consumer foods. Some countries are in the very beginning stages of the consumer food life cycle -- they can be called *developing markets*. Two scenarios exist for the developing market. Some countries may be on the verge of an economic explosion that allows a middle class to develop capable of purchasing food instead of growing it. Other countries may already have a large middle class but have erected import barriers to keep foreign foods out.

In either case, suppliers consist of one or a few firms which have high production and marketing costs because of a lack of volume-based efficiencies. The price of the product is also high. These countries may hold great long-run potential but are unlikely to yield any short run profits. Firms may enter these markets with the intention of establishing themselves early to capitalize on future sales growth.

In the next stage, countries have been industrializing for a few years and the beginnings of affluence are spreading across the population -- these can be called *growing markets*. These countries have begun to experience high economic growth rates. The improving economic conditions encourage more firms into the market, and as competition increases price usually decreases. The number of consumers who can participate in the market also increases. Markets experiencing economic growth may be easier to enter because there is plenty of room for all new entrants making the environment less competitive.

Consumer Food Exports Outpace Domestic U.S. Retail Food Sales

Index (1985=100)

Global U.S. Consumer Food Exports

Domestic U.S. Retail Food Sales

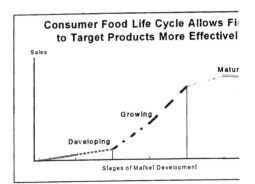

Growing markets may also consist of developed countries and advanced developing countries that are removing trade barriers. These countries have increasing consumer food demands but also existing sophisticated tastes. The potential demand and competitive conditions are similar to countries experiencing economic development. Countries that are removing trade barriers require quick action in order to fill emerging needs before other firms move into the market. In either case, the growing market represents opportunities for expansion.

Finally, sales peak in the market. Consumers cannot eat anymore food. Competition to maintain market share is intense and the potential to gain market share is slim. Research and continual new product development are necessary to stay on top of this kind of market. The *mature market* scenario occurs in developed countries. *Mature markets* require ample resources to maintain a presence and defend market share from other firms that may have different and new ideas for serving the market.

Where Do Your Resources Fit?

Each company selling consumer foods should decide in which type of markets it is most capable of thriving. A firm with a large advertising budget, established brands, a motivated sales force, and a well-staffed research and

development departme
capacity to grow an
mature market such
States. However, v
realize a better long-ru
were turned tow:
developing markets? S
have difficulty finding
serve the mature dome
find that resources cou
in less mature, *growin*
competitive pressures

For food processing f
U.S. market, the marl
driven mainly by cha
lifestyles as new st'
touting the benefits of
new flavors become p
convenient storage
methods are develc
consumer food demar
mainly from popul.
which in the United St
than one percent :
consumers spend les
income on food than :
in the world. The Uni
low food prices bec:
agriculture and fc
industries. Mean
competition is fierce i
the same reasons. Do:
sales are dominated by
with differentiated pro
population of smalle
remaining option of c
on price or in narrow

in 1994 -- and these numbers are understated because the transshipment of goods from Hong Kong are not included. FAS explored the Chinese consumer food market in depth in the May 1994 issue of *Agricultural Trade Highlights*.

Other examples of growing markets include the Philippines and Japan. Although domestic retail sales numbers are not available, the rapid expansion of supermarkets and fast food chains in metro Manila and beyond suggests a substantial middle class interested in consumer foods. U.S. exports have grown from $65 million in 1989 to $113 million in 1994, reflecting the growth potential in this market.

In other more developed countries where a middle class already exists, changes are taking place that increase the demand for consumer-oriented products. Japan is often considered a *mature market* because food consumption in general has leveled off, but the Japanese market for consumer foods hardly fits this category.

In the past, the government of Japan has retarded the consumer food market's development through restrictive import policies. The current easing of many of these restrictions puts the Japanese

consumer foods market in the growth category. Previously, domestic firms sheltered by these trade policies were able to charge high prices because of a lack of competition. Many middle class consumers were eliminated from the market because they could not afford to purchase these products regularly. Reducing trade restrictions has allowed more efficient overseas producers to enter the Japanese market, forcing down prices and inviting a larger portion of the population to partake of consumer foods. As a result, consumer food exports from the United States have grown 14 percent over the past year and this increase is expected to continue. The most recent FAS analysis of the Japanese consumer food market is in the November 1993 issue of *Agricultural Trade Highlights*.

The Most Important Step

If you want to take part in the opportunities available in growing foreign markets, the next step is to examine the markets closely and, based on your product offering and firm resources, locate the most appropriate markets. FAS can help you get started in this process. FAS can help identify current growth markets and potential developing markets for consumer foods, provide information on getting started

in international markets, and organize opportunities for participating in trade shows where exporters can make contact with potential foreign buyers. FAS has set a target for the agricultural industry to export $65 billion annually, a 50 percent increase, by the year 2000. The agency is here to help. This target can be reached only with new exporting efforts by food processors and continued perseverance by those already in foreign markets.

The author is with the Trade and Marketing Analysis Branch, FAS. Tel: (202) 720-4051, CLyon@ag.gov.

FAS Resources at Your Fingertips

AgExport Services
Trade Show Office   720-9423
Marketing Programs   690-0752
Trade Assistance and
  Planning   690-0159
AgExport Action Kit   690-3424

Overseas Offices
Foreign Agricultural
  Affairs   720-3253

Communications
Media Relations   720-7115
Publications   720-7115

Trade Policy Issues
Inter-America and
  Western Europe   720-1340
Asia, Africa, and
  Eastern Europe   720-1289
Food Safety and
  Technical Services   720-1301

Product Information
Horticultural and Tropical
  Products   720-6590
Dairy, Livestock, and
. Poultry   720-8031
Grain and Feeds   720-6219
Oilseeds and Products   720-7037
Tobacco, Cotton & Seeds 720-9516
Forest Products   720-0638

International Cooperation and Development
Cochran Fellowship Program   690-0032
Trade and Investment Program   690-1141
Professional Development Program   690-3985

Trade Policy and Market Updates

U.S. Horticultural Exports Not Yet Deriving Benefit Of EU Single Market Directive

The implementation of the European Union (EU) "Single Market".directive in its related harmonization of the EU phytosanitary regime, created new export c U.S. fruits and vegetables. Unfortunately, these potential openings have rema of reach for U.S. exporters for several reasons. First, EU production of most from the United States was at abnormally high levels in both 1993 and 1994. shipping periods have limited gains for highly perishable products such as Finally, consumer demand in the EU for fruit seems to have eased with slower e and restrictions on banana imports.

However, the outlook for the future is better, due to the EU's rapid climb c recession, and the prospect that the bumper crops of recent years are ur indefinitely. This is particularly true for U.S. fruits and vegetables that can finc the EU-produced product is unavailable or not of high quality. U.S. growe continue to pursue the EU market. For example, a delegation of Florida v growers is planning a market survey trip to several key EU member state m spring. Despite heavy competition from southern EU and North African sup selected EU posts believe Florida growers can compete effectively for the seaso1 high quality winter vegetables.

Italy Allows Imports Of U.S. Poultry Meat

After a three-year effort by FAS/Rome and FSIS, the Government of Italy sig agreement which opens the Italian market to U.S. poultry meat exports. Final a language on FSIS export certificates is expected soon. U.S. turkey and turkey should be the primary beneficiaries.

Approved U.S. Pork Plant List Established For Exports to Russia

Russia officially approved FSIS export certificates and a list of U.S. pork process facilities as eligible to export pork to Russia. As a result, U.S. pork can now Russia, accompanied only by an FSIS export certificate. The individual ship1 require pre-approval/inspection by a Russian veterinarian official. This will a pork shipments to Russia. This recent easing of requirements results from the I import protocol negotiated and signed in February 1995.

Laryngotracheitis Outbreak

A recent laryngotracheitis (LT) outbreak in Georgia is preventing poultry meat state from being exported to major markets, such as Russia, and possibly Jap Japan combined accounted for about 30 percent of U.S. poultry export value i has primary action on this matter. Any public inquiries about the LT outl directed to APHIS, Ms. Kendra Pratt (301) 734-6573.

Kenya Bans Imports Of Wheat and Corn

The Kenyan Minister of Agriculture announced an immediate 6-month ban or wheat and corn. According to the government, the ban was necessary to gi Cereals and Produce Board (NCPB) and local suppliers an opportunity to s stocks. Since the liberalization of Kenyan grain trade in 1993, high levels of agr and increasing stocks have contributed to depressed grower prices. The Unitec a significant supplier of grains to Kenya in the past. In 1993/94, the United St percent of Kenyan wheat imports, or about 400,000 tons, and 11 percent imports, or 100,000 tons.

...Trade Policy and Market Updates

Special EU Licenses Exempt Some Sales From GATT Limits

The EU is set to issue special licenses for export sales in May and June that will be valid for shipment several months after July 1 (the beginning of the new marketing year), yet not count against their GATT commitment to reduce subsidized exports. The special licenses will be limited, however, to the average quantities issued during the past three years for the same two months; that is about 870,000 tons of wheat and 635,000 tons of barley. All other export licenses issued prior to May will be invalid on July 1.

South Korea to Import Quantities Above Quota

The Korean National Livestock Cooperative Federation (NLCF) recently announced that it planns to import 27,625 tons (CWE) of frozen pork above the current quota level of 21,930 tons. This would bring total CY95 imports up to 49,555 tons. Under the original Tariff Rate Quota, the U.S. market share was 26 percent, while the EU (mainly Denmark) market share was 70 percent. The remainder of the quota was filled by Canada. The first tender for above quota amount was held on April 14 for 8,750 tons, with subsequent tenders being handled through the NLCF on a regular tender basis. The next tender will be held on or about May 10.

More Non-EEP To Russia

Knowledgeable trade sources indicate that over 15,000 tons of U.S. pork trimmings and boneless picnic shoulder meat have been exported or contracted for export to Russia recently. This business has been accomplished without subsidies and represents additional sales generated by EEP's introduction of pork cuts into Russian market.

U.S. Corn Exports to China Continue to Mount, Exceeding February Cancellation

New sales of 188,600 tons of corn to China were registered the week ending April 13, 1995. Since the cancellation of 642,000 tons in outstanding sales in February, China has made new purchases of 659,200 tons of U.S. corn. These sales bring the current total of U.S. commitments to China for the marketing year (Sep/Aug) to 2,138,300 tons.

U.S. Corn Sales To Japan and South Korea at Record Breaking Levels

U.S. corn sales to Japan and South Korea during the current marketing year September 1, 1994 through April 13, 1995 have already surpassed the previous full year export records. Total commitments to Japan now stand at 15 million tons, surpassing record exports of 14.8 million tons in 1987/88. Total commitments to South Korea now stand at 6.3 million tons, shattering the previous record export level of 5.7 million tons in 1989/90. The United States is also poised to set corn export records to both Indonesia and Malaysia, with current total commitments of 566,400 and 280,100 tons, respectively.

Thailand To Subsidize Nearly 2 Million Tons Of Rice Exports

In order to encourage exports of the winter/spring rice crop during the harvest period, Thailand initiated a program in early March that will pay US$10 per ton to exporters who export milled or parboiled rice, not better than 10 percent brokens, from April 15 to July 31. While the target export quantity under this program was 400,000 tons, over 1.8 million tons were registered by the April 17 deadline. This is the second tranche of Thailand's export subsidy program. The first installment saw the export of approximately 750,000 tons of subsidized rice, some destined to historical U.S. markets. This season marks the most aggressive utilization to date of export subsidies by Thailand, with direct payments to exporters double last year's levels.

...Trade Policy and Market Updates

U.S. Seeks Consultations With EU on Canned Fruit

The U.S. government has requested consultations with the EU Commission to discuss possible EU non-compliance with provisions of the Canned Fruit Accord (CFA). The consultations, to occur within the context of the annual canning fruit price-setting exercise, were prompted by U.S. industry concerns over alleged fraud and abuse by Greece. Independently, the EU Commission has launched a full investigation of the Greek regime, including the massive, open-ended withdrawal program for raw peaches. In setting the "world" price of canning fruit, the CFA purports to limit the amount of compensation provided Greek canners, who in theory must procure supplies of raw peaches at high minimum guaranteed prices. Aided by generous EU subsidies throughout the 1980s, Greece has become the dominant supplier of canned peaches in the world. Greek product has displaced U.S. canned peaches in many important third-country markets. Shipments of Greek product in 1994/95 (June/May) are projected to reach a record 360,000 tons.

ITC Rules No Domestic Industry Injury From Imported Tomatoes

The U.S. International Trade Commission (ITC) recently issued a negative determination in the provisional relief phase of its investigation concerning increased imports of fresh winter tomatoes. The ITC will continue with a full investigation of the petition submitted by the Florida Tomato Exchange under section 202 of the 1974 Trade Act. The Commission must make a final injury determination by July 27, 1995, and transmit its report, including any final remedy recommendation, to the President by September 25, 1995. Mexico's tomatoes compete with supplies from Florida during the first four months of the year. The Florida industry's concern heightened early this year when the devalued Mexican peso made imports very attractive. The petition was prompted by a surge of product from Mexico that resulted in triggering provisions of the seasonal Tariff Rate Quota (TRQ) under the NAFTA. The TRQ was set at 172,300 metric tons over the period November 15-February 28. Florida has asked the U.S. Government for a more restrictive form of TRQ to guard against price distortions resulting from a glut of imported tomatoes in the market.

U.S. Exports of Agricultural, Fish & Wood Products to All Countries
Calendar Years 1990 to 1995 and Year-to-Date Comparisons ($1,000)

Product	Calendar Years					January-February		%
	1990	1991	1992	1993	1994	1994	1995	Chg
Bulk Agricultural Total	20,232,083	18,348,386	19,687,248	18,593,458	18,951,466	3,322,995	4,591,374	38.2%
Wheat	3,839,037	3,292,138	4,449,324	4,664,582	4,056,007	711,156	809,327	13.8%
Coarse Grains	7,036,717	5,722,597	5,736,599	5,000,598	4,731,925	745,491	1,166,770	56.5%
Rice	801,527	753,557	726,072	771,312	1,010,548	152,567	168,875	10.7%
Soybeans	3,549,508	3,956,443	4,380,402	4,598,746	4,330,427	1,003,801	1,097,125	9.3%
Cotton	2,798,495	2,491,999	2,010,338	1,540,678	2,676,263	358,127	918,902	156.6%
Tobacco	1,441,116	1,427,631	1,650,559 *	1,306,067	1,302,745	246,447	285,023	15.7%
Pulses	353,111	268,414	191,656	213,254	280,649	30,840	42,056	36.4%
Peanuts	203,373	180,304	240,308	204,576	187,552	26,467	41,525	56.9%
Other Bulk Commodities	209,199	255,304	301,989	293,645	375,352	48,099	61,771	28.4%
Intermediate Agricultural Total	8,573,907	8,789,224	9,231,134	8,973,466	9,749,696 *	1,605,662	2,001,832	24.7%
Wheat Flour	182,956	184,256	184,317	205,729	211,248	38,540	42,855	11.2%
Soybean Meal	1,005,103	1,155,307	1,294,722	1,132,041	958,920	183,961	213,934	16.3%
Soybean Oil	312,930	222,126	376,202	363,897	525,077	72,612	178,280	145.5%
Other Vegetable Oils	394,790	418,144	502,732	543,897	671,187 *	88,038	163,596	85.8%
Feeds & Fodders (excl. pet foods)	1,572,369	1,605,732	1,722,327	1,744,163 *	1,738,454	298,570	328,947	10.2%
Live Animals	513,783	686,563 *	607,891	518,927	587,352	94,351	72,196	-23.5%
Hides & Skins	1,729,731	1,357,570	1,326,054	1,268,658	1,507,616	215,961	291,639	35.0%
Animal Fats	428,729	426,824	515,214	501,702	598,546	76,435	123,494	61.6%
Planting Seeds	588,723	671,655	675,011 *	619,359	648,614	176,103	180,075	2.3%
Sugars, Sweeteners & Bever. Bases	572,052	634,101	573,921	567,807	656,761	100,153	109,187	9.0%
Other Intermediate Products	1,272,743	1,426,946	1,452,744	1,507,288	1,645,921 *	260,938	297,629	14.1%
Consumer-Oriented Agricultural Total	10,465,615	11,967,920	13,895,994	14,911,316	16,988,134 *	2,287,750	2,692,363	17.7%
Snack Foods (excluding nuts)	530,125	633,040	829,679	1,024,643	1,101,668 *	158,645	153,657	-3.1%
Breakfast Cereals & Pancake Mix	157,882	216,802	219,762	252,993	291,979 *	41,582	42,971	3.3%
Red Meats, Chilled/Frozen	2,394,495	2,660,267	3,112,361	3,055,222	3,383,394 *	455,905	569,557	24.9%
Red Meats, Prepared/Preserved	135,998	165,101	181,562	220,038	253,621 *	37,682	34,951	-7.2%
Poultry Meat	672,888	817,913	928,464	1,100,613	1,570,414 *	187,318	272,426	45.4%
Dairy Products	328,053	462,956	793,754	857,487 *	753,257	123,791	94,758	-23.5%
Eggs & Products	101,979	143,367	139,234	139,438	164,653	22,768	23,554	3.5%
Fresh Fruit	1,486,489	1,561,053	1,683,344	1,707,147	1,953,767 *	252,286	272,610	8.1%
Fresh Vegetables	728,648	832,935	899,624	985,953	1,046,789 *	143,540	186,426	29.9%
Processed Fruit & Vegetables	1,246,753	1,394,490	1,558,121	1,639,583	1,720,891 *	241,997	292,243	20.8%
Fruit & Vegetable Juices	375,497	385,414	461,017	469,517	543,013 *	64,851	104,436	61.0%
Tree Nuts	801,120	867,704	928,531	998,246	1,106,416 *	163,772	179,517	9.6%
Wine and Beer	266,202	315,756	369,181	379,301	532,735 *	50,486	85,663	69.7%
Nursery Products & Cut Flowers	186,741	201,442	201,321	209,397 *	197,985	30,150	32,490	7.8%
Pet Foods, Dog/Cat	244,038	329,772	399,630	497,621	577,943 *	82,638	95,094	15.1%
Other Consumer-Oriented Products	808,706	979,907	1,190,410	1,374,116	1,789,607 *	230,340	252,009	9.4%
Wood Products Total	6,481,227	6,429,179	6,741,685	7,281,313 *	7,029,961	1,055,540	1,155,507	9.5%
Logs	2,388,921	2,074,432	2,140,010	2,489,560 *	2,277,981	306,226	347,251	13.4%
Lumber	2,127,895	2,203,353	2,322,491	2,449,643 *	2,428,150	380,121	395,928	4.2%
Plywood & Panel Products	769,983	735,227	847,867	906,397	944,360 *	159,677	193,952	21.5%
Other Wood Products	1,194,428	1,416,167	1,431,317	1,435,714 *	1,379,471	209,517	218,377	4.2%
Fish & Seafood Products Total (Edible)	2,776,759	3,035,383	3,353,935 *	2,959,086	3,002,265	468,634	442,316	-5.6%
Salmon, Whole/Eviscerated	666,582	436,975	681,663	583,060	518,413	17,380	15,789	-9.2%
Salmon, Canned	104,276	133,644	154,401	160,416	161,577 *	24,040	30,651	27.5%
Crab & Crabmeat	363,251	431,411	448,050 *	417,660	349,136	134,663	75,786	-43.7%
Surimi (fish paste)	N/A	N/A	367,627 *	274,322	318,850	65,269	73,206	12.2%
Roe & Urchin	289,458	389,031	421,396 *	415,319	408,963	79,539	87,104	9.5%
Other Edible Fish & Seafood Products	1,353,193	1,644,322 *	1,280,798	1,108,309	1,245,325	147,744	159,780	8.1%
Agricultural Product Total	39,271,605	39,105,530	42,814,376	42,478,240	45,689,296 *	7,216,407	9,285,569	28.7%
Agricultural, Fish & Wood Product Total	48,529,591	48,570,092	52,909,996	52,718,639	55,721,522 *	8,740,581	10,883,392	24.5%

Note: (*) Highest export level since at least 1970; N/A = not available; NA = not applicable.
Source: Trade & Marketing Analysis Branch, TEAD/TP/FAS

alues	February 1994	February 1995	Chg	October-February FY '94	October-February FY '95	Chg	Fiscal Year 1994	Fiscal Year 1995(f)	Chg
	-- $Billion --			-- $Billion --			-- $Billion --		
Feeds 1/	1.066	1.455	37%	6.031	7.045	17%	13.413	15.3	14%
Flour	0.334	0.451	35%	1.962	2.104	7%	4.228	5.0	18%
	0.083	0.084	2%	0.361	0.497	38%	0.891	0.8	-10%
Grains 2/	0.359	0.589	64%	2.159	2.743	27%	4.569	6.0	31%
	0.278	0.535	93%	1.859	2.422	30%	3.817	5.3	39%
Fodders	0.189	0.214	13%	0.978	1.059	8%	2.277	2.1	-8%
d Products	0.728	0.921	27%	3.809	4.488	18%	6.975	7.6	9%
ns	0.490	0.555	13%	2.493	2.756	11%	4.161	4.5	8%
Cakes & Meals	0.085	0.100	17%	0.514	0.490	-5%	1.013	0.9	-11%
Oil	0.040	0.113	180%	0.200	0.398	99%	0.433	0.6	39%
egetable Oils	0.049	0.079	61%	0.251	0.389	55%	0.608	N/A	N/A
roducts	0.444	0.614	38%	2.487	3.128	26%	6.320	6.6	4%
ats	0.232	0.313	35%	1.222	1.527	25%	3.206	3.4	6%
kins & Furs	0.099	0.141	41%	0.518	0.678	31%	1.423	1.5	5%
ducts	0.121	0.171	41%	0.647	0.897	39%	1.720	1.9	10%
Meat	0.095	0.143	50%	0.514	0.751	46%	1.383	N/A	N/A
cts	0.059	0.055	-6%	0.388	0.298	-23%	0.832	0.8	-4%
tured Tobacco	0.136	0.142	4%	0.567	0.648	14%	1.260	1.3	3%
Linters	0.151	0.516	242%	0.743	1.673	125%	2.306	3.4	47%
eds	0.083	0.073	-11%	0.358	0.395	10%	0.619	0.6	-3%
l Products	0.546	0.727	33%	3.188	3.929	23%	8.098	8.9	10%
pical Products	0.148	0.143	-3%	0.829	0.830	0%	1.928	2.1	9%
ucts 4/	0.537	0.620	15%	2.769	2.953	7%	6.946	N/A	N/A
eafood Products 4/	0.365	0.321	-12%	1.041	1.104	6%	2.912	N/A	N/A
lture	3.480	4.817	38%	19.047	23.331	22%	43.474	48.5	12%
ish & Wood	4.382	5.758	31%	22.856	27.387	20%	53.333	N/A	N/A

olumes	-- MMT--		Chg	-- MMT--		Chg	-- MMT--		Chg
Feeds 1/	6.664	9.927	49%	40.606	49.337	22%	88.581	N/A	N/A
	2.376	2.651	12%	14.468	13.721	-5%	31.132	33.5	8%
lour	0.085	0.140	65%	0.402	0.435	8%	1.037	1.0	-4%
	0.203	0.303	49%	1.093	1.857	70%	2.438	2.9	19%
Grains 2/	2.821	5.381	91%	18.499	26.529	43%	39.845	57.0	43%
	2.166	4.889	126%	15.850	23.409	48%	33.057	50.0	51%
Fodders	1.016	1.249	23%	5.218	5.730	10%	11.797	12.1	3%
d Products	2.505	3.456	38%	13.553	17.429	29%	24.154	30.5	26%
ns	1.845	2.487	35%	9.761	12.610	29%	16.364	21.4	31%
Cakes & Meals	0.411	0.560	36%	2.414	2.754	14%	4.859	5.4	11%
Oil	0.066	0.167	154%	0.338	0.612	81%	0.694	0.9	30%
egetable Oils	0.068	0.112	65%	0.377	0.551	46%	0.849	N/A	N/A
roducts 3/	0.192	0.295	54%	1.152	1.475	28%	2.957	N/A	N/A
ats	0.073	0.100	37%	0.394	0.490	25%	1.025	1.1	7%
ducts 3/	0.098	0.150	52%	0.529	0.773	46%	1.405	N/A	N/A
Meat	0.095	0.146	54%	0.513	0.753	47%	1.364	1.6	17%
cts 3/	0.044	0.046	2%	0.399	0.467	17%	0.467	N/A	N/A
tured Tobacco	0.022	0.024	11%	0.090	0.098	9%	0.196	N/A	N/A
nters	0.116	0.310	166%	0.582	1.055	81%	1.639	2.2	34%
eds	0.069	0.041	-41%	0.241	0.236	-2%	0.498	N/A	N/A
l Products 3/	0.463	0.568	23%	2.513	3.042	21%	6.560	7.4	13%
pical Products 3/	0.107	0.094	-12%	1.102	0.910	-17%	0.910	N/A	N/A
lture 3/	10.279	14.909	45%	60.767	74.822	23%	127.414	156.6	23%

'udes pulses, corn gluten feed and meal; 2/ includes corn, oats, barley, rye and sorghum; 3/ includes only those items measuresd in
: tons; 4/ items not included in agricultural product totals. N/A = not available.
995 forecasts (f) are based on USDA's "Outlook for Agricultural Exports," published February 22, 1995.

U.S. Agricultural Export Value by Region
Monthly and Annual Performance Indicators

	February 1994 -- $Billion --	February 1995 -- $Billion --	Chg	October-February FY '94 -- $Billion --	October-February FY '95 -- $Billion --	Chg	Fiscal Year 1994 -- $Billion --	Fiscal Year 1995(f) -- $Billion --	Chg
Western Europe	0.662	0.862	30%	3.698	4.253	15%	7.013	7.7	10%
European Union 1/ 2/	0.639	0.841	32%	3.587	4.097	14%	6.741	7.4	10%
Other Western Europe 2/	0.023	0.021	-10%	0.111	0.157	41%	0.272	0.3	10%
Central & Eastern Europe	0.025	0.032	29%	0.162	0.159	-2%	0.310	0.4	29%
Former Soviet Union	0.085	0.098	15%	0.918	0.445	-52%	1.474	1.2	-19%
Russian Federation	0.053	0.090	71%	0.785	0.360	-54%	1.095	0.8	-27%
Asia	1.390	2.255	62%	7.231	9.593	33%	17.671	21.4	21%
Japan	0.774	0.877	13%	3.864	4.156	8%	9.193	9.6	4%
China	0.047	0.343	638%	0.155	0.855	451%	0.877	1.7	94%
Other East Asia	0.408	0.627	54%	2.215	3.006	36%	5.261	6.7	27%
Taiwan	0.175	0.194	11%	0.992	1.019	3%	2.103	2.5	19%
South Korea	0.160	0.330	107%	0.826	1.391	68%	2.055	2.7	31%
Hong Kong	0.073	0.102	40%	0.396	0.592	50%	1.101	1.5	36%
Other Asia	0.162	0.408	152%	0.998	1.575	58%	2.340	3.4	45%
Pakistan	0.016	0.072	345%	0.114	0.210	84%	0.212	0.4	88%
Philippines	0.024	0.061	153%	0.214	0.262	22%	0.554	0.6	8%
Middle East	0.128	0.235	83%	0.812	1.097	35%	1.650	1.9	15%
Israel	0.050	0.057	15%	0.173	0.192	11%	0.346	0.5	44%
Saudi Arabia	0.033	0.039	19%	0.227	0.214	-6%	0.470	0.5	6%
Africa	0.191	0.242	26%	0.988	1.264	28%	2.159	2.5	16%
North Africa	0.149	0.166	11%	0.699	0.927	32%	1.438	1.8	25%
Egypt	0.042	0.089	111%	0.245	0.587	140%	0.598	1.1	84%
Algeria	0.079	0.030	-62%	0.317	0.206	-35%	0.592	0.6	1%
Sub-Saharan Africa	0.042	0.075	80%	0.289	0.338	17%	0.721	0.7	-3%
Latin America	0.593	0.635	7%	2.846	3.688	30%	7.228	7.1	-2%
Mexico	0.348	0.272	-22%	1.474	1.714	16%	4.126	3.6	-13%
Other Latin America	0.245	0.364	48%	1.372	1.974	44%	3.103	3.5	13%
Brazil	0.020	0.055	175%	0.115	0.435	280%	0.227	0.6	165%
Venezuela	0.039	0.058	49%	0.191	0.200	5%	0.401	0.4	-0%
Canada	0.373	0.415	12%	2.061	2.408	17%	5.248	5.7	9%
Oceania	0.033	0.042	30%	0.215	0.283	32%	0.497	0.6	21%
World Total	**3.480**	**4.818**	**38%**	**19.047**	**23.332**	**22%**	**43.474**	**48.5**	**12%**

Note: 1/ EU-15 (historical and forecasted figures include the newest member states of Austria, Finland and Sweden).

2/ FY 1995 forecasts are unofficial estimates, however they will be replaced with offical Department figures in May 1995.

Source: FY 1995 forecasts (f) are based on USDA's "Outlook for U.S. Agricultural Exports," published February 22, 1995.

Value Of U.S. Dollar Against Major World Currencies
Daily Spot Quotations & Monthly Averages

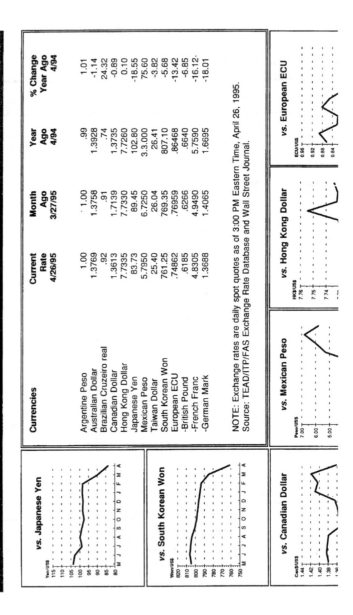

Currencies	Current Rate 4/26/95	Month Ago 3/27/95	Year Ago 4/94	% Change Year Ago 4/94
Argentine Peso	1.00	1.00	.99	1.01
Australian Dollar	1.3769	1.3758	1.3928	-1.14
Brazilian Cruzeiro real	.92	.91	.74	24.32
Canadian Dollar	1.3613	1.7139	1.3735	-0.89
Hong Kong Dollar	7.7335	7.7330	7.7260	0.10
Japanese Yen	83.73	89.45	102.80	-18.55
Mexican Peso	5.7950	6.7250	3.3.000	75.60
Taiwan Dollar	25.40	26.04	26.41	-3.82
South Korean Won	761.25	769.35	807.10	-5.68
European ECU	.74862	.76959	.86468	-13.42
-British Pound	.6185	.6266	.6640	-6.85
-French Franc	4.8305	4.9490	5.7590	-16.12
-German Mark	1.3688	1.4065	1.6695	-18.01

NOTE: Exchange rates are daily spot quotes as of 3:00 PM Eastern Time, April 26, 1995.
Source: TEAD/ITP/FAS Exchange Rate Database and Wall Street Journal.

NTIS Order Form
For FAS Subscriptions

U.S. DEPARTMENT OF COMMERCE
Technology Administration
National Technical Information Service
Springfield, VA 22161

For RUSH Service—Call 1-800-553-NTIS
RUSH service is available for an additional fee.
To order subscriptions, call (703) 487-4630.
TDD (For hearing impaired only), call (703) 487-4639.

☎ (703) 487-4630
or Fax this form to (703) 321-8547
To verify receipt of your Fax order,
call (703) 487-4679.

▷ Payment

☐ Charge my NTIS Deposit Account _ _ _ _ _ _

Charge my   ☐ VISA   ☐ MasterCard   ☐ AMERICAN EXPRESS

Account No. |_|_|_|_|_|_|_|_|_|_|_|_|_|_|_|

Exp. _____ Cardholder's name _____
                                          (Please print)

Signature: _____
                        (Required to validate all orders)

☐ Check/Money order enclosed for $ _____
                                          (Payable in U.S. dollars)

▷ Ship to Address

Date _____

Company _____

Attention _____ Title _____

Last Name _____ First Initial _____

Suite or Room Number _____

Full Street Address Required _____

City _____ State _____ ZIP _____

( ) _____ ( ) _____
Telephone number   Fax number

Please PRINT or TYPE

Return Policy: To inquire about the NTIS return policy, please call the NTIS Subscription Section at (703) 487-4630.

Single Copies: To order single copies, call our Sales Desk at (703) 487-4650.

Subscription Price Schedule
Foreign Agricultural Service (FAS) Publications

No. of Subscriptions	Order No.	Titles	Domestic	Foreign	Total
_____	PB95-970600LJX	Agricultural Trade Highlights (12 issues)	$ 50.00	$ 80.00	_____
_____	PB95-970700LJX	Tropical Products (Coffee, Tea, Cocoa, Spices Essentials Oils) (4 issues)	22.00	44.00	
_____	PB95-970800LJX	Cotton: World Markets & Trade (12 issues)	60.00	112.00	
_____	PB95-970900LJX	Dairy, Livestock & Poultry: U.S. Trade & Prospects (12 issues)	78.00	174.00	_____
_____	PB95-971000LJX	Dairy Monthly Imports (12 issues)	50.00	80.00	
_____	PB95-971100LJX	Livestock & Poultry: World Markets & Trade (2 issues)	14.00	22.00	
_____	PB95-973900LJX	Dairy: World Markets & Trade (2 issues)	14.00	22.00	
_____	PB95-971200LJX	All 28 Dairy, Livestock & Poultry reports	136.00	278.00	
_____	PB95-971300LJX	Grain: World Markets & Trade (12 issues)	70.00	140.00	
_____	PB95-971400LJX	World Horticultural Trade & U.S. Export Opportunities (12 issues)	70.00	140.00	
_____	PB95-971500LJX	Oilseeds: World Markets & Trade (12 issues)	76.00	152.00	_____
_____	PB95-971600LJX	U.S. Planting Seed Exports (4 issues)	38.00	96.00	
_____	PB95-971700LJX	Sugar: World Markets & Trade (2 issues)	14.00	16.00	
_____	PB95-971800LJX	Tobacco: World Markets & Trade (12 issues)	66.00	154.00	
_____	PB95-971900LJX	World Agricultural Production (12 issues)	75.00	120.00	
_____	PB95-973400LJX	Wood Products: International Trade & Foreign Markets (5 issues)	42.00	92.00	
_____	PB95-973500LJX	Monthly Summary of Export Credit Guarantee Program Activity (12 issues)	50.00	80.00	
_____	PB95-973600LJX	U.S. Export Sales (52 issues)	175.00	320.00	
_____	PB95-973700LJX	AgExporter Magazine (12 issues)	34.00	42.00	_____

Prices*

Prices are subject to change.
The NTIS Subscription Section (703) 487-4630 can provide pricing verification.

* Prices include first-class delivery for domestic; airmail delivery for foreign.

GRAND TOTAL [_____]

Important Notice to Readers --

Agricultural Trade Highlights is published monthly
National Technical Information Service (NTIS) for $:
to foreign addresses (air mail). Prices are subject to ch
number (PB95-970600LJX).

- ■ To order by phone, using VISA, MasterCard
- ■ For rush service (available at an additional
- ■ To order single copies, call (703) 487-4650
- ■ The TDD number (for hearing-impaired per
- ■ Orders can also be mailed to: U.S. Departm
  National Technical Information Service, Sp
  orders.

This publication is a product of the Trade and Ec
Service, U.S. Department of Agriculture, Room 3059-
20250-1026. Questions on the subject matter of thi:
at (202) 690-0553.

Agricultural Trade Highlights Staff includes:
Production Assistants
  Paula Lane
  Anne Player

Note: The United States Department of Agriculture
on the basis of race, color, national origin, sex, religi
familial status. (Not all prohibited bases apply to all
alternative means for communication of program infor
contact the USDA Office of Communications at (2(

To File a complaint, write the Secretary of Agricult
D.C., 20250, or call (202)720-7327 (voice) or (202)
employer.